E

AND

WATER

JOHN METCALFE

Printed and Published by
John Metcalfe Publishing Trust
Church Road, Tylers Green
Penn, Buckinghamshire

—

—

First Published October 1988

—

ISBN 1 870039 18 1

—

Price 25p

—

CONTENTS

BLOOD AND WATER

BLOOD AND WATER

But one of the soldiers with a spear pierced his side, and forthwith came there out blood and water.

John 19:34

I. Observe, Firstly, The Apostle Testifies to the Blood of Christ

'FORTHWITH came there out blood' This is the only reference in the gospels to 'blood' at the cross. Neither Matthew, Mark, nor Luke mentions the blood of Christ at the cross*. Only John refers to the shedding of blood in the narrative of the crucifixion. It is in the epistles that the doctrine is revealed; the gospels, however, provide the narrative. First, in the synoptic gospels, Matthew, Mark, and Luke, the crucifixion in and of itself. Secondly, in John, of the mystery that is hidden at the cross, yet disclosed in figure and sign in the unfolding events of the crucifixion.

*'Christ Crucified'; John Metcalfe. See Order Form for details.

Hence, uniquely, John points to the blood of Christ, not anticipating the doctrine in the epistles, but bringing to light signs otherwise veiled in the gospels.

The blood shed at the cross is referred to as that of Jesus; of Christ; of the Lord; of Jesus Christ; of God's own Son, and as the blood of the Lamb. No wonder Peter calls it 'precious' blood. If of Jesus, then of one holy, harmless, undefiled, touched with the feeling of our infirmities, yet unique, peerless, doing the works which none other ever did, receiving the testimony of heaven beyond comparison. Jesus is a name towering over time, above the creation, beyond all generations, the name of the mediator between God and man, the only name given under heaven among men whereby they must be saved. His blood.

The blood of Christ: that is, of God's Anointed. All who ever came before him, anointed with oil, were but types and figures, shadows of whom he is the substance. It is true that in sundry ways and divers manners God spake in times past unto the fathers by the prophets, but in these last days he hath spoken in his Son, that is, in Christ himself. God did ordain a covenant by Moses, through angels, but, finding fault with it, afterwards brought in a new, an everlasting, an eternal covenant through the Anointed. Aforetime God reigned in Israel by the king David, whom Samuel had anointed, but now God reigns through Christ, anointed with the Holy Ghost, in mount Zion, from the heavenly glory. David died, but Christ abides for evermore.

David reigned over an earthly kingdom which perished, but Christ reigns with an everlasting dominion over the world to come which shall never perish. In times past the succession of dying priests ministered figurative sacrifices which could never take away sins. But now Christ, a priest for evermore, having obtained eternal redemption for all his people by one sacrifice for ever, infallibly brings through time into eternity, through darkness into light, through dishonour into glory, through this world into the next, every last one of God's elect, each one purchased by blood, all those given to him by the Father before the beginning of the world, leading them to glory when the world is no more. For this he was anointed. For this he is called the Christ. For this Christ shed his own blood.

Everything that is true, all that was treasured up, each promise that shall be fulfilled in the purpose of God, concerning the Anointed, the Christ, is settled upon Jesus. The heritage seen in those aforetime anointed with oil, becomes the spiritual inheritance to which Jesus was born. He is the anointed king, the Holy Ghost is given without measure to him in the administration of his priesthood, the anointing is poured out with and upon every utterance of his prophetic ministry. Hence he is called Jesus Christ. It is his blood that was shed. If so, such a blood shedding, such a death at the hands of Israel, must have a significance of incalculable effect upon every man born of woman throughout all generations.

The blood that was shed at the cross is called the blood of God's own Son. It is the LORD's blood. Then there is a mystery about it, a holy, awesome uniqueness that stills heaven, that makes the earth to hold its peace, and causes all mortal flesh to keep silence before him. Deity is in the matter, divinity infuses the substance, the Godhead has an interest, investing the blood of God's own Son with a singularity, a heavenliness, a spirituality, that reaches to eternal verities, to everlasting truth, to endless settlements, to things imperishable, immortal, unconditional, in their effect upon all those for whom that blood was shed. It is the LORD's blood. 'The church of God, which he hath purchased with his own blood.'

Finally, the blood to which John points at the crucifixion is called 'the blood of the Lamb'. That is, the Lamb ordained before—and slain from—the foundation of the world. Then, before the Fall. If so, anticipating the Fall: meeting it, answering it, triumphing over it, bringing in at the end more than ever the hatred of Satan, the malice of man, or the wickedness of demons, ever lost in the beginning. For, 'Where sin abounded, grace did much more abound.' And much more abound through the blood of the Lamb. The Lamb is hinted in Adam, brought forth to Abel, sacrificed by Noah, offered up through Abraham, prefigured at the commandment of Moses, set forth as sacrificed by day and by night, year in and year out, so long as the sun and moon endure. The Lamb is revealed from Genesis, fulfilled in the gospels, declared by the epistles, and consummated in the Revelation. The Lamb brings in the atonement, the Lamb sets forth the substitution, the Lamb is God's cry to man, and man's answer to God: 'Behold the Lamb of God, that taketh away the sin of the world.' No wonder, I say, no wonder that Peter called this—the blood of Jesus, of Christ, of Jesus Christ; the blood of the Lord, of God's own Son; the blood of the Lamb—'precious' blood; peerless, beyond price, outside of every scale of values save that of the divine estimation of the heavenly sanctuary, of the holy place made without hands, abiding for evermore.

The blood of Christ is said to be the blood of the new testament. That is, a covenant has been brought in which does not depend on the will of man or rest upon works. This covenant has nothing to do with human priesthood, carnal ordinances, worldly sanctuaries, professions of the dead letter of scripture, attendances at the world's 'churches', conformity to man's authority in religion or anything else short of what was in the beginning. The new testament is a covenant ordained entirely of God, mediated absolutely by the Son, ratified unconditionally by the blood of Christ, and administered wholly by the Holy Ghost from heaven. This is a testament in which the Father and the Son undertake the entire responsibility to save a people and to bring that salvation spiritually to the inward man with powerful, heavenly, everlasting and divine effect. It is a covenant wrought entirely of God, in which God is the saviour, and men are the saved; in which Christ is the life, the Spirit is the power, and the Father and the Son are the church: 'The church which is in God the Father and in the Lord Jesus Christ.' In this covenant salvation has been already fully secured by blood—'it is finished'—of which that blood is witness in heaven and on earth, the Spirit himself bearing witness also. This is a covenant in which the Father is made known by the Son through the Spirit, in light, life, liberty and love, and, in consequence of this, God is sought and worshipped in spirit and in truth by every one of the true worshippers in the heavenly sanctuary, which is the house of God, the church of the living God, the pillar and ground of the truth. All this, every part of it, besides the resurrection from the dead and the everlasting glory to come, is secured by nothing but the blood of Jesus.

The blood of Christ is said to justify, and to have secured the sentence of justification upon every one of God's people —in and of itself—from the beginning of the world to the end of it, when it was shed. Then, the righteousness of God is unto all those for whom the blood of Christ was shed, when it was shed, so that because of this alone—though they be ungodly sinners—they are accounted righteous in the sight of God, with a righteousness not their own, imputed to their account just as much as if they themselves had wrought it*. God's righteous judgment, in this world or that to come, now or before the throne of judgment in the last day, God's righteous judgment, I say, can find no fault with the righteousness imputed to debtors because of the blood of Christ. On account of that shed blood they have been justified with an everlasting righteousness in view of the resurrection from the dead in the day of judgment at the end of the world.

By the blood of Christ, God, who was angry with sinners on account of their transgressions, is propitiated and rendered amiable towards them, being thoroughly appeased by the blood shed on their behalf. By the blood of atonement their transgressions are forgiven, their sins are covered, and God no more imputes iniquity unto them. Their sins are remitted, they are pardoned, their souls are ransomed, and they are reconciled to God for no other cause than the shedding of the blood of Christ.

The people of God have redemption through his blood. That is, by virtue of the shedding of Jesus' blood they are already in possession of an accomplished redemption. Hence the elect are said to be redeemed from the law and its curse; redeemed from all iniquity; redeemed from the fall, their sins, and their trespasses; redeemed from the king of terrors, the last enemy, death itself; redeemed from the grave and

*'Justification by Faith'; John Metcalfe. See Order Form for details.

from hell; and, seventh and finally, the people of God are said to be redeemed with an everlasting redemption which is absolute and unconditional. All this, by nothing but the blood of the Lamb. They did nothing; they neither had nor have anything to do: indeed, they can do nothing. All is wrought by the blood of Christ: no wonder, then, that Peter declares this blood to be priceless, calling it 'the precious blood of Christ'.

II. Observe, Secondly, The Apostle Bears Witness to Blood 'and Water'

Water, in this place, is a sign of the Holy Ghost, secured for all those for whom Christ's blood was shed, when his blood was shed: 'Forthwith came there out blood and water.' All was settled, assured, and established by his death. There the sheep were purchased, and there the Spirit, without whom they could not be brought to faith, was secured for them so that they—and none other—should be brought to faith. Hence of others it is said, 'Ye believe not, because ye are not of my sheep', Jn. 10:26. Then, the sheep believe because they are his sheep, that is, from eternity, by purchase, and before believing. All his sheep—'I lay down my life for the sheep'—were purchased by his blood, and by his death the Spirit was secured for them, and assured to them, to bring them from death to life, darkness to light, unbelief to faith, and from destruction to glory. At his death it was certain: hence 'forthwith' out of his side came forth blood and water, water signifying the Holy Ghost secured for all the elect by the death of Christ, as it is said 'This spake he of the Spirit', John 7:39.

Now notice what the apostle John does not say:

1st. He does not say, Blood without water

The profession of many, if not most, modern 'evangelicals' —as they think of themselves—is in fact a profession in the dead letter; of blood, yes, but that blood has never been applied *to them* by the Holy Ghost: it is blood *without* water. But the apostle does not say, Blood without water. He says, Forthwith came there out blood *and* water. However, whilst these profess the blood of Christ, it is evident from their dead, hard and cold unspirituality, from their worldliness, that no water ever proceeded to them from the death of Christ. Of this sort are the outward letter traditionalist Brethren, together with certain fringe groupings of sectarian Baptists, supposing that God is pleased with an outward form and not the inward spirit, with their traditional bath of water and not the baptism of the Holy Ghost, and with the formal sign of a cup—or an hygenic tray of tiny glasses—of unfermented grape juice as opposed to the spiritual reality of the blood of his own Son by the Holy Ghost from heaven.

Corrupt Brethren and unregenerate Arminian sectaries are fond of 'claiming' salvation, and 'taking God at his word', as they call it, by which they mean presuming on scripture truth into which the Holy Ghost never led them, and to which God by no means gave them spiritual title. All their salvation is in the dead letter; what they read about the blood of Jesus is what they claim, but the Spirit never applied it, the Holy Ghost did not reveal it to them, they are void of 'water' with the blood, and hence they are at once dry, barren, and without fruit. It is not the blood that they have:

the scripture that describes the blood is all that constitutes their easy-believing claims.

David knew nothing of such formal, outward, traditional and dead-letter religion, for he cried to the living God, 'Purge me with hyssop', by which he meant the vital application of the Holy Ghost himself, crying, 'Take not thy Holy Spirit from me'. He did not, he could not, and he would not purge himself; he did not, he could not, and he would not commit that purging to men. God was the one who must purge David, and so he cried with all his heart. David knew the blessedness of the man unto whom the LORD imputed not iniquity. Then he knew the curse of that rotten religion in which men claim that their iniquity is not imputed to them on the strength of the mere profession of the bare text, when God has done nothing to them whatsoever. It is the grace of God that brings salvation, not the lame feet and withered arm of free will that go and fetch it. Salvation is of the LORD, not of man. Wherefore? Because 'forthwith came there out of his side blood *and* water', in that 'our gospel came not unto you in word only, but also in power, and in the Holy Ghost, and in much assurance.'

2nd. Neither does John say, Water without blood

Under this heading swarm other sorts of pestilential troublers of the church of the living God, namely those who have no doctrine. Everything with such tumultuous persons is a claimed present experience, a presumed immediate revelation: they have no objective foundation, no grounding in truth, no basis outside their own existence whatsoever, they rest upon nothing but sand, and belch forth nothing but hot air. Justification by faith has no place with this kind of legion—for they are many—they rejoice to knock down the walls of salvation, to unhinge the gates of praise, to break asunder Zion's bars of iron, and to say of that which was once laid down by Christ and the apostles at the beginning 'Rase it, rase it, even to the foundations thereof', Psalm 137:7. These join hands with the papists over the ruins of Protestantism, frothing out their own shame, squalling together with joy in a shared 'experience' of what they commonly call 'love', but which is in reality the overturning and destruction of everlasting truth, the very essence of enmity against God.

Such presumptuous dreamers as these, full of fermenting talk of the spirit, yet know nothing of the Spirit of truth come to glorify Christ. They assert waters to swim in, but they themselves are filthy. They despise and detest the apostolic foundation of the Christian church, building on clouds without water which float across the present imagination of their unstable souls. They care not how a man should be just with God, they have no doctrine: justification, propitiation, remission, reconciliation, redemption, ransom, mean nothing to them, less than nothing; they spurn the doctrine as divisive, as deadening; they trample the doctrine of the gospel under their feet, and thus in them is fulfilled the saying 'Give not that which is holy unto the dogs, neither cast ye your pearls before swine, lest they trample them under their feet, and turn again and rend you.' The reformers gave them what was holy, pearls came to them by inheritance from the great divines, but, rising against the truth of Protestantism and of recovery, they have trampled the blood of Christ, and rent the messengers of the LORD of hosts, Hebrews 10:29, Matthew 21:35.

Such apostates from the faith once delivered to the saints are all vaunted and foaming claims, they are full of great swelling words, they are replete with busy doing and working, as they call their feverish and uncontrolled activity. With them it is all mystic leading, 'prophecies', fanatical full-time, all special revelations, everything is centred on what they do, upon themselves, on healing, inspiration, and ecstasies which they claim to receive. That is, all their talk is of 'water'. Never of blood, according to the doctrine of God's holy word. But they shall proceed no further, for the immutable truth which they oppose is summed up in this scripture, John 19:34, 'forthwith came there out *blood* and water'.

3rd. Neither—in point of time—is it said, Blood before water

As if believing were one thing, but receiving the fulness of the Spirit another thing: that is, with such people, to have faith in the blood of Christ is first, and common to all believers, but to receive the fulness of the Holy Ghost, to experience the 'rivers of living water', is a further, special experience, remaining open to all who have believed. This is a far more serious error than at first appears. It is the early, Wesleyan methodist 'second blessing' teaching, based on the fundamentally erroneous notion that all that there is of the Holy Ghost for the elect was not secured and made certain by the death of Christ, but that it depends upon the will and progress of man to attain to the 'second' blessing. Transmuting through various 'holiness' movements, this error reappeared under the guise of Pentecostalism in which it was taught that though all are believers who are brought to faith in Christ's blood, only those have 'the baptism of the Holy Spirit' who receive a second experience, distinguished by 'speaking in tongues'. This is nothing but deception and the loosest of errors, leading to a loss of self-control and the danger of possession, the very opposite of the fruit of the Spirit. Many have been snared in this false teaching, a teaching clean contrary to the ancient paths, the old landmarks, the soundness of the great divines, of the Reformation, and of the unalterable doctrine and experience of the church of God.

This loose error, resurfacing in these last times as the Charismatic delusion, has carried away multitudes, including such pillars—as some thought—as Martyn Lloyd Jones. Like a popular tide, the delusion has carried all before it in the Anglican and papist sects, uniting them in one excited movement irrespective of their distinctions, and, of course, the dissenters and Brethren were not slow to follow what was popular and fashionable, having long been carried off in a swollen tide of togetherness by the glamour of American mass evangelism.

The Charismatic delusion, acknowledging believers in the blood of Christ, but holding forth a second experience, marked by the—falsely so-called—'baptism of the Spirit', creates an elite class of the spiritually deluded. To 'authenticate' their induced 'experience' this special class invent tongues—a false and fleshly copy of what had appeared by the Holy Ghost under the apostles in the early church, the deception being created by nothing but the letting go of all self-control—in which the abandoned dupes babble incoherent nonsense like raving imbeciles.

Another version of the same error is to be found under the cloudy disguises of the 'Honor Oak' Christian fellowship—so-called—and that of the 'Little Flock' of Watchman Nee—as he called himself—partial rapturists all, holding two classes of 'believers', namely, 'children', who merely believe in Christ's blood, and 'sons', that is, themselves, who in their pride suppose that they are a kind of elite in consequence of their special 'enlightenment'. Thus the church is not what it is as a result of the death of Christ: it is divided into two, the ordinary believers, mere 'little children', and the specially initiated 'grown sons', namely the 'little flock', who secrete their divisive heresy, so well-cloaked with high sounding words of evasion.

In all these errors, whether 'second blessing', the false wresting of the 'baptism of the Spirit', the Charismatic delusion, the Honor Oak heresy, or that of the Little Flock, falsely so-called, they depend for their existence upon the presumption of special attainment, a particular experience—after believing—marking out an elite class, a distinct group, *and not upon the death of Christ for the whole church.* But the truth is, everything was purchased for all by Christ in his death, and the Spirit himself was fully secured and certain to all believers for no other cause than that he died. Everything is in the death of Christ, and that is what all these errors undermine. They undermine the Lord in his death. There can be no 'second experience', no such wresting of spiritual baptism, no distinction between 'children' and 'sons' depending on human attainment. Christ brought in and attained everything, securing all to every believer immediately upon his death, including the baptism and fulness of the Holy Ghost, certain to every one that believeth when brought to believe. 'Forthwith'—mark that *forthwith* —'came there out blood and water.' Not blood *before* water.

4th. Nor—in point of time—does John say, Water before blood

Under this head is discovered the teeming multitude of the Arminian strivers, Hagar's seed indeed, all children of the bondwoman, though diverse in their family branches and often adept at disguising their origins with a cloak of scripture texts, much like to sheep's clothing.

The term 'water before blood' precisely indicates the inversion of scripture perpetrated by those who would rob the Almighty of his strength, God of his majesty, the deity of all sovereignty, the blood of its efficacy, and the Spirit of his power, by predicating a general grace for all, and the Spirit—the 'water'—universally 'pleading' with everybody, kindly, please, to have pity on an impotent, dying, saviour, the whole issue being dependent on the good will and kindness towards God of those men who choose to yield to him. That is, of salvation by works, the initial move of which is, by definition, unaided by the Spirit, since those who yield to the Spirit, and others who continue to resist him, do so from nothing but their own unaided resources. And is this called grace? Yes, by them it is.

How can they call it grace? By saying that the 'water' of the Holy Ghost is shed equally on all mankind, in order to persuade men to accept the blood of Christ. Then, '*water before blood*'. How is this grace? Because, they say, without the Spirit, men would not come. See how this hypocrisy begs the question! If without the Spirit they would not come, then from whence the power to receive the Spirit, so that—thereafter—they might come? And why do some receive this Spirit and some reject him, if it be not that some are better—or less fallen—than others? And if so, their works, springing from a better, unaided heart, enable them to receive what the wickedness of others makes them refuse, namely, that power by which they might be drawn for salvation to the blood of Christ. This not only makes the Spirit dependent entirely on the good will of man, it makes him impotent to overcome the ill will of man, elect or not. That is, it exalts salvation by works, and dethrones salvation by grace, dependent for effectiveness upon nothing other than the relative goodness of some men over against others.

This ancient heresy postulates a general atonement equally for all, and a universal giving of the Spirit so that everyone may attain to it. A general atonement, but men must receive the Spirit individually to come thereto. Then, that atonement actually saves none: it only makes possible the salvation of all. The blood justifies none: it merely makes justification a possibility for those that add to it their own willingness. This overturns the election, tramples upon grace, diminishes the Fall, laughs at depravity, mocks the judgment, despises the saviour, trades the shekel of the sanctuary for trickster's values as light as air, and it makes Father, Son and Holy Ghost impotently dependent upon the good will of—some sovereign—men, in order to salvage the nebulous suggestion that God has not been entirely devoid of some part in man's gracious efforts without which nobody would have been saved at all.

Though not the branches, this is the very root of popery. This is the strength of antichrist, and the doctrine by which a false church with a pseudo-gospel has overwhelmed the appearance of the true throughout the denominations and sects of Christendom. This is the real exposure of modern evangelism, of bastard Calvinism, and of the swarming 'evangelicals' by whom Satan has deceived the whole world. Nevertheless, the foundation of God standeth sure. He who looks at the proud swelling waves, the shifting sea and the boiling froth of Christendom, swiftly sinks into confusion and despair. But he who looks up steadfastly to him who is over all, to the Rock of our salvation, abideth still.

Whoso discerns this vile and rotten system, whether in the papist mass house, the Anglican steeple house, the Baptist tabernacle, the Methodist chapel, the Brethren hall or the Presbyterian law-court, will find all these branches drawing sustenance from the same tap-root, as does that American mass evangelism which feeds them, with a subtle, deluding flattery of 'water before blood' blinding the eyes of the simple. But he who has been taught the plague of his own heart, who has been brought to fall utterly before the majesty of Almighty God, who knows by revelation that nothing but an effectual atonement, a justification by blood, can save him, and none but the quickening Spirit, the Holy Ghost, can bring him to believe upon that finished work once wrought, even he shall inherit the blessing, and shall be shown the way to the city.

5th. But the wording which stands immutable in holy writ is this: 'Blood and water'

The words 'blood *and* water' indicate a concurrence, a harmony of the twain. The fact that 'forthwith' came there out of the side of the dead saviour 'blood *and* water', reveals that immediately upon his death all the benefits of that death for those for whom he died were already secured. Not only all the worth and value of his precious blood, but *at the same time*—'and'—all the absolute and infallible certainty of the person and work of the Holy Ghost necessary to bring those for whom he died to everlasting glory. This is the gospel in a sign. Anything otherwise signified is 'another gospel'. And though we, or an angel from heaven preach any other gospel unto you than that which we have preached unto you, let him be accursed.

As we said before, so say I now again, If any man preach any other gospel unto you than that ye have received, let him be accursed. For do I now persuade men, or God? or do I seek to please men? for if I yet pleased men, I should not be the servant of Christ. But I certify you, brethren, that the gospel which was preached of me is not after man. For I neither received it of man, neither was I taught it, but by the revelation of Jesus Christ. Which is what no hireling pastor, nor any of the multitude of academically taught and appointed ministers, neither yet the salesmen droves of self-seeking evangelists, can ever say. But by the grace of God, the revelation of Jesus Christ, and the interior teaching of the Father, subject to the doctrine of the apostles, I can say it, no man making me a liar, or making my speech of nothing worth. And if I should say otherwise, I should be a liar like unto them, that is, a liar against the grace and revelation of Jesus Christ which appeared to me as my salvation these thirty-five years ago.

A further indication implied in the words 'forthwith came there out of his side blood *and* water', is that just as Christ's death in and of itself at the moment in which he died secured the everlasting and unalterable redemption of all his people, together with the fulness of the person and work of the Holy Ghost absolutely assured to bring them to faith and to glory, so also these two things—blood and water—come simultaneously and fully in and to the experience of each believer. That is, just as the blood of Christ is wholly communicated and assured to the faith of the believer when he believes, so the Holy Ghost is wholly communicated and assured to the faith of the believer when he believes. If the one, then the other.

The application of the blood of Christ to the conscience of the believer is spiritual, just as believing is the result of the quickening of the Spirit. Both were secured for the elect when Christ died, and both are applied in their entirety to the elect when they believe. That is, the blood of Christ is spiritually applied when the Spirit takes of the things of Christ and reveals them, as it is written, 'When he, the Spirit of truth, is come, he will guide you into all truth: for he shall not speak of himself; but whatsoever he shall hear, that shall he speak.' He hears that one who was purchased by blood at the cross is now to be called by grace, and, hearing, he reveals that blood to the called: 'He shall glorify me: for he shall receive of mine, and shall show it unto you', Jn. 16:13,14. Hence, as the blood, so the Spirit is given unreservedly to all who believe, when they believe. This experience is seen is Acts 10:44, 'While Peter yet spake these words, the Holy Ghost fell on all them which heard the word.' It was simultaneous, the word of the cross, and the baptism of the Holy Ghost, the 'blood *and* water'.

In another place this is referred to as 'The washing of water by the word', Eph. 5:26, and answers to the prayer of Jesus to the Father, 'Sanctify them through the truth; thy word is truth'. This prayer has its fulfilment in the words 'Sanctification of the Spirit and belief of the truth', II Thess. 2:13, a simultaneous experience in the saved, just as it was a simultaneous sign in the Saviour, John 19:34 'Blood *and* water'.

It follows of necessity that as there is no 'second blessing' in relation to the blood once shed, so there is no 'second blessing' in relation to the shedding of the Holy Ghost. The blood, once shed, is thereafter applied for ever. And the 'water'—of the Holy Ghost—once shed, shall 'abide with you for ever', John 14:16. The Holy Ghost no more comes with two, or any number, of successive 'blessings', than does the blood. What applies to the blood, applies to the Spirit. What holds good with the one, holds good with the other. It is 'blood *and* water.' That is the doctrine, and all experience must be judged by and subject to it; the doctrine must never be judged by or subject to experience. The truth is, 'He shall not speak of himself: he shall testify of me', and, if so, Christ's doctrine is the criterion, not men's ranting of what they claim the Spirit has done for or by them: it is 'Testify of *me*'. How could subjective claims be the criterion when 'Thy word is settled in heaven'? When, 'He shall not speak of himself'? And if he, the Holy Ghost from heaven, puts Christ and his doctrine over all, not speaking of himself, who are these, with their great swelling words of vanity?

What must be grasped is what no carnal man will ever yield by nature, because the religion—whether heathen idolatry, legal Judaism, or apostate Christianity—of all natural men is that which postulates the initiative and latent goodness of the human race towards God. This, however, is no religion at all, it is the lie of Satan, the god of this world, blinding the minds of them that believe not. It is the ancient liar flattering man, 'Thou shalt not surely die'. But die man did, dead man is, and die man shall: and what works can be performed from the grave? These dead can do nothing save weave Arminian fantasies from the thread of nature drawn by the prince of darkness, and never more so than when under an evangelical persuasion, well glossed over with scriptural texts, and greased with a larding of Calvinistic opinions. Grace, and grace alone, will teach a man, and that by the inward revelation of the Holy Ghost, teach a man, I say, that the Spirit—without whom blind and dead sinners cannot believe—that is, the 'water', was obtained, absolutely, unconditionally and eternally, for all for whom Christ died, when he died, John 19:34.

The work of the Holy Ghost is not dependent on the will of man, any more than his person is subject to human sovereignty. Were that so, Christ's work would be ineffectual. Jesus' blood would have redeemed none: it would merely have made redemption a possibility. What would then make redemption an actuality, would be the sovereign elect will of man calling for and subsequently receiving the otherwise impotent Holy Ghost. Make it an actuality, that is, provided man deigned to continue in that Spirit till the end. As to Almighty God—though he sent the Son, and bruised him, causing the shedding of his blood, at the cross —given that the redeeming blood was, after all, not really redeeming, but possibly redeeming, dependent on man accepting the Spirit, why, then God is not Almighty. It is man that is almighty. And what kind of a doctrine is this? I will tell you: it is the doctrine that fills the mouth of the beast speaking great blasphemies; it is the doctrine of the beast with two horns like a lamb, speaking like a dragon, Rev. 13:11-14. And it is the very spirit of antichrist, whether expressed through heathendom, Judaism, Christendom, Arminianism or Calvinism.

But Christ's work is a certain work, springing from the absolute commandment of Almighty God, infallible in its predestined consummation. And therefore the Spirit's work is an assured work, springing from an everlasting redemption absolutely achieved by the shedding of blood at the cross, sovereign in its immutable majesty. It is absolutely assured that all those—the 'many'—for whom Christ shed his blood must and shall come into faith and enter glory, because that blood was shed. 'Moreover whom he did predestinate, them he also called.' And who were the predestinated? even those whom he foreknew in time, looking back into eternity, those chosen from everlasting, the elect. These, and these only, he called, and called effectually. 'And whom he called, them he also justified: and whom he justified, them he also glorified.' On this account, and none other, it can be said, and it is said, 'Who shall lay any thing to the charge of God's elect? It is God that justifieth', Rom. 8:30,33.

Here is a certain work of the Spirit, not a conditional work. A certain work, referring back to the work of the Son. And the work of the Son is a certain work, not a conditional work. A certain work referring back to the work of the Father. Here all is immutable, absolute, everlasting. Here is an unconditional salvation in blood and water. This is the death knell to all Arminianism, in all its branches, such as popery, American evangelism, the Charismatic delusion, easy-believism, bastard Calvinism, and all who love and believe a lie. Because the Spirit was obtained for all for whom Christ died, when he died, and obtained to everlasting glory, being assured to all those for whom the blood was shed, in the sovereign will and almighty majesty of God. 'I will'—mark that, *will*—'send him'—him, not a series of experiences—'unto you.' 'That he may abide with you for ever.'

III. Thirdly, Observe the Significance of Water in John

The word 'water' occurs twenty-four times in the gospel according to John, and is used on most occasions as a figure of the Holy Ghost: 'This spake he of the Spirit.' Out of the fulness of the Spirit given to his people appears an abundance for all the spiritual seed of Abraham from out of the twelve tribes of Israel, and for all those brought into the new testament under the doctrine of Christ and of the twelve apostles. The holy city possesses twelve gates and twelve foundations, having the names of the twelve tribes and of the twelve apostles of the Lamb respectively, answering to the twenty-four elders for whom Christ obtained and the Father sent of that fulness that flowed from the pierced side of the saviour.

The twenty-four occurrences of the word 'water' in John are grouped together—more or less—in connection with a series of seven incidents, namely, first, the water of baptism, John chapter one; the water made wine, John chapter two; the water in the well, John chapter four; the water in the pool of Bethesda, John chapter five; the rivers of living water, John chapter seven; the water in the pool of Siloam, John chapter nine; and, seventh, the water in the basin, John chapter thirteen. All the references to water fall into these groupings, directly or indirectly, save that which summarises and gathers up all, the eighth, namely, the water which came from his pierced side, John chapter nineteen.

This apostolic ministry is what the wise man calls 'Giving a portion to seven, and also to eight', Ecc. 11:2. The sevenfold perfection of the work of the Holy Ghost for the redeemed people of God appears as already sealed, perfected and assured to all eternity by the blood of the everlasting covenant. The redeemed are seen by John variously and typically in the book of the Revelation as, for example, twenty-four elders, as one hundred and forty-four thousand (twelve by twelve by one thousand); just as they appear in the twelve tribes and under the twelve apostles respectively.

The work of the Spirit, the sevenfold sealer of heaven, towards those already redeemed by the blood of Christ, to find them out, call them forth, and bring them in, is seen in the seven lamps of fire burning before the throne, which are the seven Spirits of God. Here are the seven eyes of the Lamb, likewise called the seven Spirits of God sent forth into all the earth, that is, to bring in the perfect number of all the elect—already purchased by blood—with infallible and absolute certainty, which is what appears conclusively in the book of the Revelation.

Here the voice of the Son of God is as the sound of many waters; he speaks, the Spirit carries forth his voice, and the dead that hear shall live, and must live, because he has already purchased as many as the Father gave to him with his own blood. This is called justification unto life, and answers to 'blood and water'. Again; the Lamb, whose blood had redeemed all God's elect from the foundation of the world—given unto him to redeem and afterwards to call—in consequence leads them to living fountains of waters. This is his work: to redeem them by his blood before they knew him; to lead them to the living waters that they might know him. Here also is 'blood and water'.

Once more: the redeemed, having been purchased by blood when they were dead in sins and afar off, thereafter are shown a pure river of water of life. They are *shown* it, they have not to seek it, or strive for it, his blood secured it, and it is a perfect provision for the new man for all eternity. This river issues forth from the house, first up to the ankles, then to the knees, thence the loins, at each thousand cubits length, that is, at each divine (three) leading into the completeness (ten) of Christ and his work, unto the measure of the stature (ankles, knees, loins, head) of the fulness of Christ, which are waters to swim in indeed. But from whence issue these waters? From under the altar. That is, 'blood and water'.

By the perfection of the work of the Son, through the perfect work of the Spirit, the redeemed are perfectly united to the Father and the Son. This union shall never be broken, for it stands in an everlasting communion in eternal life by one Spirit with God in three persons, Father, Son, and Holy Ghost.

By the same Holy Ghost all the elect are assuredly led to walk in one Spirit, to be spiritually minded, to mind the things of the Spirit, to dwell in the Spirit, to be indwelt by the Spirit, and to live in the Spirit, waiting until, hoping for, and hasting unto the coming of the Son of God from heaven, for the resurrection, the glory, and the world to come whereof we speak. All this, for every child of promise redeemed by blood, for all the church of God which he hath purchased with his own blood, for every heir of faith justified by Christ's death, all this, I say, is absolutely and unconditionally assured to all the seed, because 'Forthwith came there out of his side blood and water'. Mark that: 'blood *and* water'.

The perfect work of the Holy Ghost is assured and certain because of the death of Christ, as the substitute of his people, having finished the transgression, having made an end of sins, having made reconciliation for iniquity, and having brought in everlasting righteousness. Then, having justified every last one of the elect. If so, having glorified the entire church, for, 'Whom he justified, them he also glorified'. When he died. The full range, the perfect conclusion, of all the work of the Spirit was there and then secured to every heir of faith. 'He that believeth on me, out of his belly *shall* flow rivers of living water.' 'Shall'—not may: it is unconditional—because of the effectiveness of his death. This is the blessedness of the man, who, believing upon Christ, hath his transgressions forgiven, his sins covered, and to whom sin is not imputed. Believing in such a saviour, he rejoices with joy unspeakable and full of glory, being lost in wonder, love, and praise. This is called 'rivers of living water'. It proceeds from a well within, springing up into everlasting life. Why? Because the blood of Jesus Christ, God's Son, hath cleansed from all sin, for ever, to which the Spirit bears everlasting witness in every single one of the ransomed people. This is called, 'blood *and* water'.

The work of the Spirit—sent forth from the Father—is to bring every one to Christ whom the Father gave to him from eternity, and whom he purchased with his own blood in time. This work is as infallible as it is invariable, though all the dogs bay and grudge against it without the city, and every bondchild and all bastard Calvinists gnash their teeth with envy and rage to the contrary even at the very gates. The work begins, firstly, with the sounding of an alarm; this results in the awakening of the sinner; the work goes on to the conviction of sin and of the wrath to come; afterwards follows a quickening into life; then next the turning of a real conversion; sixthly, there appears the gift of faith; and, lastly, the granting of repentance unto life.

This work proceeds in consequence of a sound regeneration, together with the baptism of the Holy Ghost, and results in a washing, yea, an anointing, followed by a continual renewing, proceeding to the sealing, and, seventhly, to the earnest of the Spirit setting Christ before and bringing the glory in to every child of promise. The power of Jesus' resurrection, the hope of glory, the savour of the world to come, the sense of eternity, and, above all, the light and glory of Christ from on high, illuminate and quicken the inward parts of the faithful, as days of heaven upon earth, to the praise of the glory of his grace, world without end, Amen.

All this is secure and certain to every one that seeth and believeth the Son. That is, to all the poor in spirit, all the meek, every mourner, all those who hunger and thirst after righteousness, those weary and heavy laden, who weep now, and who know affliction by the rod of his wrath. These are called babes, the ignorant, the weak things, the ignoble, the offscouring, the base things, the things that are not, the foolish of this world. These are the called: that no flesh should glory in his presence. By these God confounds the wise, the scribes, the hirelings, the priests, the teachers, the lawyers, the doctors, the noble, the things that are, the strong, the prudent in this world, the mighty, the substantial, the highly educated, the legalists, the 'righteous'. By these babes, I say, God brings confusion to the exalted, sending the rich empty away, despised, whilst in their place the poor are exalted and filled with good things. And wherefore? That he might have all the glory, that no flesh should glory in his presence, so that the scripture might come to pass in reality: 'He that glorieth, let him glory in the Lord.'

Glory in the work of God: 'For of God are ye in Christ Jesus': that is, ye are not in Christ Jesus of yourselves, or of your own will, or of your own fancy choice, which is nothing but false faith and easy-believism, the imagination of the heart; no, but, 'Of God are ye in Christ Jesus', who—in fact—are in Christ Jesus. It is not of works, lest any man should boast.

Glory in the work of the Spirit: 'Who of God is made unto us': it is not of our making him anything to ourselves, nor by any act of our own will or volition. It is his taking the things of Christ and showing them unto us, proceeding from the Father, glorifying Christ, not speaking of himself, testifying of the Son, witnessing, leading, filling all the true chosen children of Abraham.

Glory in the work of Christ: 'made unto us wisdom, both righteousness, sanctification and redemption': he is made by revelation our wisdom within, the light of the glory shining in our hearts through the face of Jesus Christ in a mystery. We have no righteousness, only filth and total depravity, he is our righteousness before God, an everlasting righteousness, imputed to every one that believeth, through faith in his blood. He is our sanctification, 'Christ in you, the hope of glory', and our redemption, our lot and inheritance secured in Christ to everlasting ages, when this present world is no more.

Glory in the work of God: so that all the work and all the glory might be of God, and nothing of man, for 'Cursed is he that trusteth in man', and, 'Cease ye from man, whose breath is in his nostrils: for wherein is he to be accounted of?' But, 'Blessed is the man that trusteth in the LORD.' That is, that all the glory might go to God in salvation, even to Almighty God, to Father, Son, and Holy Ghost.

Whereof God has given witness, advertising us, saying, according to holy writ, 'One of the soldiers with a spear pierced his side, and forthwith came there out blood and water'. This blood and water came out of his death, fulfilling in the Lion of the tribe of Judah, the Root of David, the true proverb, 'Out of the strong came forth sweetness'. And that is what we are seeing recovered and restored to the heirs of promise, even in our own day. Though the sign thereof be no bigger than a man's hand, we see it clearly, it is evident, and in consequence, we call to all who watch for the opening of the floodgates of heaven: 'Prepare: get thee down; that the rain stop thee not.' Amen and Amen.

JOHN METCALFE

MINISTRY BY JOHN METCALFE

TAPE MINISTRY BY JOHN METCALFE
FROM ENGLAND AND THE FAR EAST
IS AVAILABLE.

For Tapelist please contact the John Metcalfe Publishing Trust, Church Road, Tylers Green, Penn, Buckinghamshire, HP10 8LN.

Owing to the increased demand for the tape ministry, we are unable to supply more than two tapes per order, except in the case of meetings for the hearing of tapes, where a special arrangement can be made.

Book Order Form

Please send to the address below:-

		Price	Quantity
A Question for Pope John Paul II		£1.25	......
Of God or Man?		£1.45	......
Noah and the Flood		£1.20	......
The Red Heifer		£0.75	......
The Wells of Salvation		£1.50	......
The Book of Ruth (Hardback edition)		£4.95	......
Psalms, Hymns & Spiritual Songs (Hardback edition)			
The Psalms of the Old Testament		£2.50	......
Spiritual Songs from the Gospels		£2.50	......
The Hymns of the New Testament		£2.50	......
'Apostolic Foundation of the Christian Church' series			
Foundations Uncovered	Vol.I	£0.30	......
The Birth of Jesus Christ	Vol.II	£0.95	......
The Messiah	Vol.III	£2.45	......
The Son of God and Seed of David (Hardback)	Vol.IV	£6.95	......
Christ Crucified (Hardback)	Vol.V	£6.95	......
Justification by Faith (Hardback)	Vol.VI	£7.50	......

Name and Address (in block capitals)

. . . .

. . . .

. . . .

If money is sent with order please allow for postage. Please address to:- The John Metcalfe Publishing Trust, Church Road, Tylers Green, Penn, Bucks, HP10 8LN.

Tract Order Form

Please send to the address below:-

		Price	Quantity
The Two Prayers of Elijah		£0.10	......
Wounded For Our Transgressions		£0.10	......
The Blood of Sprinkling		£0.10	......
The Grace of God That Brings Salvation		£0.10	......
The Name of Jesus		£0.10	......
'Tract for the Times' series			
The Gospel of God	No.1	£0.25	......
The Strait Gate	No.2	£0.25	......
Eternal Sonship and Taylor Brethren	No.3	£0.25	......
Marks of the New Testament Church	No.4	£0.25	......
The Charismatic Delusion	No.5	£0.25	......
Premillennialism exposed	No.6	£0.25	......
Justification and Peace	No.7	£0.25	......
Faith or presumption?	No.8	£0.25	......
The Elect undeceived	No.9	£0.25	......
Justifying Righteousness	No.10	£0.25	......
Righteousness Imputed	No.11	£0.25	......
The Great Deception	No.12	£0.25	......
A Famine in the Land	No.13	£0.25	......
Blood and Water	No.14	£0.25	......
A Testimony to John Metcalfe's Ministry from Penang and Singapore		Free of charge	......

Name and Address (in block capitals)

. . . .

. . . .

. . . .

If money is sent with order please allow for postage. Please address to:- The John Metcalfe Publishing Trust, Church Road, Tylers Green, Penn, Bucks, HP10 8LN.

THE MINISTRY OF THE NEW TESTAMENT

The purpose of this 32 page A4 gloss paper magazine is to provide spiritual and experimental ministry with sound doctrine which rightly and prophetically divides the Word of Truth.

Readers of our books will already know the high standards of our publications. They can be confident that these pages will maintain that quality, by giving access to enduring ministry from the past, much of which is derived from sources that are virtually unobtainable today, and publishing a living ministry from the present. Selected articles from the following writers have already been included:

Eli Ashdown · John Bunyan · John Burgon
John Calvin · Donald Cargill · John Cennick · J.N. Darby
John Foxe · William Gadsby · William Huntington
William Kelly · Hanserd Knollys · James Lewis
Martin Luther · John Metcalfe · Robert Murray McCheyne
Alexander—Sandy—Peden · J.C. Philpot · J.B. Stoney
Henry Tanner · John Vinall · George Whitefield · J.A. Wylie

Magazine Order Form

Name and Address (in block capitals)

. . . .

. . . .

. . . .

Please send me .... current copy/ies of The Ministry of the New Testament.

Please send me .... year/s subscription.

I enclose a cheque/postal order for £ ....

(Price: including postage, U.K. £1.75; Overseas £1.90)
(One year's subscription: including postage, U.K. £7.00; Overseas £7.60)

Cheques should be made payable to The John Metcalfe Publishing Trust, and for overseas subscribers should be in pounds sterling drawn on a London Bank.

10 or more copies to one address will qualify for a 10% discount

Back numbers from Spring 1986 available.

Please send to The John Metcalfe Publishing Trust, Church Road, Tylers Green, Penn, Bucks, HP10 8LN

All Publications of the Trust are subsidised by the Publishers.